BLOOD ON THE GROUND
Elegies for Waiilatpu

PRAISE FOR
BLOOD ON THE GROUND

There are many ways to tell a story. The Whitman Story, a complex and tragic 168-year old drama has been told many ways, but never better than by Lenora Good who uses poetic verse to relive that cataclysmic day in November 1847. Her sensitivity and empathy for the characters of the Whitman calamity is apparent; her story is compelling.

—SAM PAMBRUN (Great-great- or Great-great-great-Grandson of Pierre C. Pambrun who was the head of Fort Nez Perces when the Whitmans arrived in 1836)

In her richly riveting verse narrative of events leading up to the Whitman massacre and away again after the killings were done, history buff Lenora Rain-Lee Good introduces us to a complex cast of characters, including Joe Lewis, the half-breed agitator who convinced the Cayuse the Whitmans were deliberately poisoning them, and five Cayuse, who surrendered to stand trial—and were hanged. Good gives us the story as those who lived it may have spoken. Poetry has a way of getting straight to the heart of things, making this a story you will not soon forget.

—MARJORIE ROMMEL, Poet Laureate, Auburn, Washington

Poet Lenora Good has penned tender verses that evoke images of a tragic event in Oregon's history. She captures the confusion, the loss, the grief of the Whitmans and others shocked or killed or taken captive that day. And she brings us the winds that wash the rye grasses still today at Waiilatpu, where dreams were shattered on a cold November day in 1847. A good story—or poem—ought to memorialize and help us remember. Lenora's *Blood on the Ground* does that with clarity and warmth.

—JANE KIRKPATRICK, award-winning author of *The Memory Weaver*

Here is history as it was lived by the people who made it--written in their own voices, raw and alive, passionate, angry, frightened, despairing. What happened at the Whitman Mission is a microcosmic experience of the settling of the West; the clash of alien cultures, blind devotions, terrors, hatreds, misunderstandings. In Lenora Rain-Lee Good's masterful recreation, we live through the horror, experience the aftermath, and bury the dead. And here too, is one of the great lessons of history: all the people here, slayers and slain, villains and innocents—in the end, they were all victims.

—STARR MORROW, author of *From One Side to Another* and *A Once and Future Place*

An unexpected treat! Lenora takes us back to difficult times in the Pacific Northwest and reintroduces us to intense emotions applied to history that can come only from the heart.

—Philip H. Red Eagle

I am not a poetry reader but thoroughly enjoyed the narrative and historical facts presented in *Blood on the Ground*. Ms. Good does a masterful job of weaving the Native American side of the Whitman tragedy into a compelling storyline.

—Ned Eddins, historian and author, www.TheFurTrapper.com

Ms. Good's *Blood on the Ground* tells the story of the killings at the Whitman Mission in 1847 in southeastern Washington State. You can read the twenty-two poems, enjoy the dance of language and image, get a fuller understanding of the emotions and beliefs of the participants, and broaden your understanding of that moment in history and the tragic consequences. But there is a larger message. Whenever people as individuals or as nations meet without regard for another world view, meet with subjugation as the goal rather than respect and tolerance, there will be "blood on the ground." Just look around at the world today.

—Jane Roop, award-winning poet

To a poet, the highest compliment is the pang of blood-curdling jealousy as I wish I had written this spectacular book of poems. The dance of cultures and blood captivated me from first page to last.

—Ralph-Michael Chiaia, poet, *The Sacred Calendar*

Leave it to Lenora Good to craft a prismatic narrative poem from the raw material of a historical massacre. She seamlessly weaves facts and imagination in order to explore, from a variety of conflicting perspectives, the sad story of catastrophe in the Oregon Country. The dominant pioneer myth has been challenged many times, but seldom with the grace and subtlety of *Blood on the Ground*.

—Fain Rutherford, Northwest poet

In *Blood on the Ground: Elegies for Waiilatpu*, Lenora Good shares the story of the Whitman Massacre and a land where "the grit of sand, rye chaff, wheat dust blows through the valley like history, like memory, rubs the stone to a high sheen, slowly polishes the names away." Fortunately for readers, Lenora Good has captured the voices of those whose names have faded in this remarkable collection of narrative poems. Told from multiple perspectives, the poems are rich in detail and research. As the poet says of the massacre, "None escaped to tell it quite the same." And no reader will escape unchanged after reading Good's elegies.

—Maureen McQuerry, author of *The Peculiars* and *The Time Out of Time* series

REDBAT BOOKS ✣ PACIFIC NORTHWEST WRITERS SERIES

Blood on the Ground
Elegies for Waiilatpu

Lenora Rain-Lee Good

redbat books
2016

Copyright © 2016 by Lenora Rain-Lee Good

All rights reserved. This book or any portion thereof may not be reproduced or used in any manner whatsoever without the express written permission of the publisher except for the use of brief quotations in a book review.

Printed in the United States of America

First Trade Paperback Edition: August 1, 2016

ISBN 978-0-9971549-1-7
Library of Congress Control Number: 2016945916

Published by
redbat books
2901 Gekeler Lane
La Grande, OR 97850
www.redbatbooks.com

Text set in Garamond Premier Pro.

Cover Artwork: "146" by David Memmott
Book design by Kristin Summers, redbat design | www.redbatdesign.com

Acknowledgments

I thank my three Sisters of the Heart and sister poets Starr Morrow, Marjorie Rommel, and Kitty Todorovic-Eppard, for their unstinting help, encouragement, and shoulders when I needed to cry.

Many special thanks to Jane Roop, Tara Pegasus, Richard Badalamente, and Sam Pambrun, for their comments, suggestions, and encouragement. Sam is much closer to the history than I ever will be, and his thoughts and suggestions are very, very much appreciated.

National Park Service Ranger Renee Rusler deserves, and receives, an equal amount of gratitude for her patience in answering all my questions. Stephenie Flora of the Oregon Pioneers (www.oregonpioneeers.com) generously and quickly answered any question I put to her. And to Seth Dalby, Archives & Records Manager of the Catholic Archdiocese in Seattle, Washington, I truly appreciate your help and patience. A huge "Thank You" to you all!

I am grateful to all the historians, professional and amateur, who so diligently collected and published the facts as they found them about the Whitman Massacre. Special thanks to the National Park Service for putting the entire book *Marcus and Narcissa Whitman and the Opening of Old Oregon* by Clifford M. Drury online. Acknowledgment must also go to Narcissa Whitman and Eliza Spalding who kept journals and wrote letters (and to the families who saved and later shared those letters), and to Catherine, Elizabeth, and Matilda Sager who lived through and wrote about the massacre. (The initial outbreak of violence occurred on 29 November, 1837. Three children, Helen Mar Meek aged 10, Louise Sager aged 6, and one infant died of measles, or neglect, during captivity.)

Many others gave encouragement, comments, and support. You know who you are, and I thank you, deeply and sincerely.

Not all histories agree; therefore, the rangers at The Whitman Mission use Clifford M. Drury as their final authority.

Lastly, but oh-so-importantly, I acknowledge you, dear reader, for having the trust in me to invest your money and your time to purchase and read this book.

Thank you.

Lenora
Lenora.good@icloud.com

Whenever people as individuals or as nations meet without regard for another world view, meet with subjugation as the goal rather than respect and tolerance, there will be "blood on the ground."

—Jane Roop, award-winning poet

Depiction of the Whitman Mission (Waiilatpu) in 1843
Courtesy Eon Images

A Lesson in History

A marble slab, names carved deep as sorrow,
laid atop the Great Grave more than 100 years
ago, holds those bones found upon the prairie—
ten men, two boys, one woman—keeps them
from rising, reassembling, and coming back to life,
to the Place of Rye Grass, "Waiilatpu."

The grit of sand, rye chaff, wheat dust blows through
the valley like history, like memory, rubs the stone
to a high sheen, slowly polishes the names away.

Each witness to the massacre saw something different—
swore, hands upon the Holy Bible,
that what they saw was true.
None escaped to tell it quite the same.

Mary Ann Bridger worked in the kitchen where
Marcus and her brothers talked till the killing
began. She escaped, through the door
—or the window, you decide—to tell Narcissa of the horror.

Joe Meek and the Oregon Volunteers came later,
found the bones pulled from the shallow grave
scattered across the prairie a mile and more.

Narcissa, known by the light auburn hair still attached to her skull.
Marcus, by his gold tooth. The men gathered the bones
they could find, placed them in the grave (now called
the Great Grave) upturned a wagon and covered it with dirt
where it protected them for 50 years.

Witnesses, all dead—the dust of their journals, their letters,
their memories, joins the dust of their bones.
What is lost is gone forever; what remains is treasure.

Though oft-told, it is doubtful Meek found and reburied
the bones of his daughter, Helen Mar. She is buried deep
in the old cemetery, undisturbed by man or beast.

The Ghosts of Waiilatpu still race through
the valley, still carry the grit of dust and rye and wheat,
polish their grave marker to high sheen
as they sing their lamentations.

The Disappointments of Narcissa Whitman

Sagebrush, Narcissa Whitman once wrote,
is offensive both to the sight and smell.

Today, her Waiilatpu Mission is covered in
emerald-green grass, neatly trimmed, with brick

outlines of all the buildings—none of which
show doors to allow for people and ideas

to get in, get out, get mixed, get taught.
The stone that marks where her baby drowned

is now far from the river's shore. Little Alice Clarissa,
gone in a heartrending moment, leaving behind only

grief and unrelenting guilt, lies somewhere below the hill
where Narcissa kept vigil from her kitchen window

and where the wild, purple rye still grows. Buried three times
Narcissa now lies covered by marble, at rest

with Marcus, her husband, her arms eternally reaching
for her daughter, alone in a grave forever lost.

Did Narcissa answer the call of God when she
badgered Doctor Marcus to marry her, to travel

to the Oregon Country, to minister unto the Indians?
Or did she answer the call of her own romance,

the *idea* of saving souls, of doing good?
One of two white women to first cross the

Rocky Mountains, her place in history
was assured even without the anger of the Indians

at the whites, who kept coming and coming
bringing with them devastating diseases.

Today, the site of the Whitman Mission
is a beautiful, green, and tranquil park where

no millstone turns; no smith hammers hot metal,
shaping horseshoes or pots or nails or wagon wheel rims.

Today, no classrooms fill with young, eager minds;
Cayuse and Nez Perce seldom come to call.

The river has moved far from where Alice Clarissa drowned
and in the distance fields of wheat and vineyards

flourish, as does the traffic, but the Mission remains;
the millpond, filled with turtles and geese, is quiet.

The solitude brings deer to eat the windfall apples from
the replanted orchard the Indians destroyed.

Might Narcissa have been happier in The Dalles
with more rain and less sagebrush?

A question with no answer.

Today, many enjoy the perfume of sagebrush, consider it beautiful,
and like the Indians, burn it with sweet grass in ritual cleansings.

Narcissa would not understand. She would still think
sagebrush offensive to both sight and smell.

Questions on Waiilatpu

What secrets will be revealed in future years
when the slab, worn smooth by the wind, overgrown
by sagebrush, wild rye and wheat, is once again found?

Will new people think the stone an altar to an old god,
that the bones beneath it are those of ancient sacrifice?
How will they re-imagine, re-write, re-tell our history?

How much of our history is true?
How much is romanticized story passed down
through the ages? Which story sells? Do we really care?

Will the sagebrush re-seed itself
in memoriam?

Dreams Die, Marcus Said

Beloved, Marcus said, I have decided
our dream is dead. Tomorrow, I shall talk
with the Chiefs and the Elders. If they
so desire, we shall sell our beloved
Waiilatpu to the Catholics and move
our family to The Dalles.

I shall ask them to let us stay
until the children are well. I shall
promise them we will leave
as soon as they have recovered.
Think, my dearest, you shall have
white women for company,
schools for the children, I shall
doctor the ill, and you shall be
a proper housewife.

Why, my Narcissa, why do you cry so?
Surely, this is the will of the Lord.
We shall be surrounded by friends.
We will have room for your sister
Jane; and, dear wife,
I promise, in our new home,
there will be no sagebrush.

Our plans were but a dream,
Beloved, and now we wake.

I Have Sorrows, Narcissa Said

I am sorry we came to Waiilatpu,
this place of rye grass! Here
there is too much sagebrush
and too little rye.

I grieve my home is gone,
destroyed, burned,
my clothes ripped,
thrown upon the winds,
my china, my beautiful
china, lies smashed
in the ice cold mud.

I am sorry my children—
where are my children? I call,
but they do not answer.
I hear Alice Clarissa crying,
but no, she is dead
these many years.

It is dark, and I am so cold.

All I want is to bring the Indians
the Blessings of our Lord Jesus Christ.
Why do they choose ignorance?
Why do they blame us for their illness?

It is that evil Joe Lewis
who lies, stirs the pot of
hate, and laughs.

It is so dark! I am so cold!
Why am I covered with mud?
Why is my blood on the ground?

That Joe Lewis

He is full of hate. I am thinking
he is full of jealousy for Madame Whitman,
that she will not be his *petite amie*.

Enfin, he has a care in his wolfish heart
for some of the young boys, *les metis garçons*.
I think he does not much care for the young girls.

He tells me, "Nicholas Finlay, you take the twins
and that David Malin Cortez and you ride
to the fort before the killing starts."

The twins, they are happy to be gone from the
classroom, but that Davey, he cries.
He is scared. He does not want to go back to his *maman*.

He wants to go back to the classroom,
to Madame Whitman, and to his sisters,
his *metis soeurs*.

The priest, he torments Davey. Tells him
he will go back to his Indian *maman*
and grow up to be a good Indian boy.

His *maman Indienne* burned him
and threw him into the trash.
Davey fears the priest will sell him
for a slave. I hope not.

He is *un bien garçon*.

"Finlay," the priest calls, "do you want to Confess?" I should. I have sinned mightily. But I too fear the priest.

And God.

The Wolf of Joe Lewis

No one wants me.
Not whites, not reds,
not blacks. No one. I hate
them all. Especially white women.
The wolf of hate grows within me.

My mother is red, my father is black.
Protestants call me a child of Satan.
The Black Robes accept me.
For a while they feed me, clothe me
shelter me. They calm my wolf
—for a while.

I traveled west with the Black Robes;
they to save souls, I to kill whites
—especially that woman, Narcissa Whitman.
She does not belong with red-skinned people.
I hate her, though we have never met.
I hear she teaches the People *her* ways,
her language, *her* god. She feeds the whites
as they continue to come.

My wolf snarls at thought of her.

The Black Robes left me in Boise.
Too full of hate, they told me, to travel
with men of God. I walked alone, with only
my wolf for company.

I arrived at the Place of Rye Grass
footsore, cold, in rags. Too ignorant
to know they succor their own death,

they fed me, clothed me, gave me a job.
Too little, too late.

Wolf's hunger grows.

With Joe Stanfield and Nicolas Finlay,
we lie, spread rumors about the fair
Narcissa and her doctor husband.
We stir the pot until emotions boil, until
the People rise up. And kill!

My wolf feeds.

Narcissa, her husband, some children
and friends—all dead, and Wolf
is finally sated, for now.

I steal away when no one watches,
a feral grin bares my fangs.

I, Tomahas, Tell You This

Enough! We tire of the white medicine man
who brings more whites, who brings
more measles he does not cure.

He will not learn our ways but
insists we learn his.
Today he learns that a medicine man
who practices bad medicine
—a medicine man who causes death
or allows death as he has done—
must pay our price.

Today my chief and friend Tiloukaikt
and I force our way into the kitchen
where we are not allowed
but where Doctor Marcus stands.
While my Chief engages Doctor Marcus
in talk, I step behind the white man,
raise my tomahawk and bring
it down upon his head.

The Bridger girl screams, runs out
the door. A Sager boy draws his pistol
and dies.

Doctor Marcus will practice
no more bad medicine.

I say to you, burning sagebrush
will cleanse the land
and remove his vileness.

I, Tomahas, tell you this.

Father Brouillet's Dreams Turn to Nightmares

As I child, I dreamed of martyrdom for the Holy Church,
for the Word of God, for my staunch beliefs. Now I face it:
I find I have no stomach to drink from that bitter cup.

Agitated to the point of violence, the Cayuse rose against
the Whitmans, killing thirteen. Those who escaped the killing
are locked away, crowded and frightened.

Had the Cayuse waited one more day....

Joe Stanfield assures me I am safe; the Cayuse
will not harm me. I have no choice but to trust him
and trust in my Lord.

Stanfield, alone when I arrived, knelt in the icy mud,
washed the dead, wrapped them in shrouds.
Alone, he dug the long and shallow grave.

Together, we lower the thirteen cold bodies into the hole
where they lie side by side, ten men, two boys, one woman.

I sprinkle them all with holy water,
baptize each one in the Name of the Father, the Son,
and the Holy Ghost, then

I sprinkle the first dirt upon each of the dead, and leave
Stanfield to cover them as I ride away into the rain.

The clean perfume of sagebrush masks the stench of death.

Who Cries for Helen Mar?

Sister? Mary Ann? Where are you?
Why have you not returned?
I thirst.
I'm cold.
Mary Ann, why am I alone?

Davey, sweet David Malin, are you here?
Won't someone please come?
Mother? Father?

I smell sweet grass and sagebrush.
Did you bring it, Davey?
I'm so cold. It's so dark.

Why am I alone?

Marriage After the Massacre

"Ken ye cook?" a man of the Old West
might ask. "Yes," she might reply, and ask
"Have you property, a house,
a job, a horse you treat well?"

As the Oregon Country opened, marriage
was more often a matter of mutual
survival. Marriage for love, for romance,
is a relatively new phenomenon.

Did you marry for love?

"Do you? Will you?"—and it was done.
If no preacher was within reach, they'd
take care of that later—unless she
was Indian, or mismated to one.

If Indian, a warrior could buy her
from her father for so many horses
or Hudson's Bay blankets—or, if
she was from an enemy tribe,
he might just steal her.

She might go. She might
    —or might not—stay.

When Five Crows, a chief of the Cayuse
tricked Lorinda Beweley, offered her protection, then
took her for a bride, and she was refused rescue by Father Brouillet;
Five Crows was perplexed—why would she ask,
let alone beg and cry—to be returned to her people?

Frank and Edward son of Tiloukaikt, asked for
and received, Susan Kimball and Mary Smith—

and were considerably surprised by Susan's copious tears
and brave Mary's angry, flashing eyes.

> *Were you considered brave*
> *because you didn't weep at your marriage?*

Were these girls given, or sold for a price?
If so, what was paid and who paid it?
We know they were taken, coerced perhaps,
offered as sacrificial lambs to spare other hostages.

> *Did your father arrange your marriage?*
> *Did he get a good price? How good?*
> *Do you know what it was?*

A long month later, the ransom was paid,
all the hostages rescued. How long did it take
for the stolen women to return to normal?

Susan and Lorinda married white men, and
produced large families. But what happened to
feisty Mary Smith? Did she ever forgive?
Did she ever find love, or marry again?

> *After one or three or twelve children*
> *are you still married?*

What purpose did these marriages achieve?
Once the women were ransomed,
the marriages were dissolved.

Joe Stanfield proposed marriage to the widow
Mrs. Hays. She said no. He explained marriage

to him would save her life, and the lives
of her children.

After that, they told everyone they were married,
but her four-year-old slept between them.
I wonder how long?

    Do you love your spouse?

Who Remembers David Malin Cortez?

David Malin Cortez
soon you will forget
your white name.
Soon you will be reunited
with your mother
who never wanted you
anyway.

She will give you a new name
—your Indian name.
You will no longer have
books to read
or lessons to write.
You will forget your English.

Indians do not need Bibles
and in fact should not have
them. I will keep your
Testament and use it properly.

You will soon forget your
brothers, your beloved
sister, Helen Mar Meek
—all the family you once had.

You will also forget vile
Doctor Whitman, who stole
your heritage, spread measles
among your people
and did not cure them.

You will forget those
who loved you, and whom

you loved. Soon, my son,
you will be forgotten
by history—even by me.

Mary Ann Bridger Speaks of John Sager

John and I desired to marry.
We waited only for the right time
to discuss it with Mother and Father
Whitman and to visit my father,
Jim Bridger, to seek his blessing.

My John was a hard worker
and Mother taught me well
the proper way to keep a house.
I knew we would be very happy...

till that day, that horrible day
when Tomahas and Tiloukaikt forced
their way in, angry and
yelling. They killed Father
and John, and later killed Mother, too.

They destroyed our happy family
as surely as the apple trees Mother planted—
chopped down, broken, to grow no more.

I tried to help the sick children
but it was not allowed, and they died
of neglect: my sisters,
my brothers, my family. All dead.

When rescued, I was sent to a home
in Oregon City, where I was colder
because of the constant damp than
ever I was at Waiilatpu.

Separated from those I knew and loved,
I am alone now in sorrow and failing

health, my lungs slowly fill—I feel
the cold more every hour.

Will John greet me in Heaven?

The Second Burial

Winter winds carry a ghostly song
across the frozen rye, gather a twist of lost smoke
and bring it, an offering, to those who silently ride along.

Joe Meek and the Oregon Volunteers came
to find buildings that might have offered shelter
gone—burned to ashes, blown by the winds.

In silence, they find the grave ripped open by wolves,
the bones gnawed, scattered upon the plain. The men
collect them, give them back to the earth, to long, silent peace

in a deeper grave marked by an overturned wagon
covered with dirt and reverence, love and off-key
songs, but no tears. The time for tears is past.

Joe Meek, a mountain man, carefully collects the bones,
the small bones of a child, scattered about the ground
and hears her weeping in the winds, singing her ghostly song.

He wonders if the bones belong to Helen Mar, his daughter.
He burns sweet grass and sagebrush, the only offering of
love he can give her. He never knows Helen Mar sleeps

undisturbed in yon cemetery. Brave men, quiet men,
they turn a wagon over the grave,
cover it with dirt and prayers,

for the dead, for the survivors, for themselves.

In Remembrance:
Burn Sweet Grass, Sage, and Holy Cedar

1. I, Tomahas, Now Known as the Murderer, Speak

For two years we lived with our women
for two years we lived with our children
for two years we lived with our people
and then the chiefs came, the elders came,
and we talked.

We five loved our wives
we five hugged our children
we five forbade sadness
as we saddled our best horses and
rode away from our desert and home,
our bunch grass and sagebrush,
our dry and warm sun.

The chiefs rode beside us
the elders rode behind us
we five did not ride alone
to meet the U.S. Marshal
Joe Meek, beside the mighty river.

He asked us why we surrendered.

I answered for us all,
Does a Savior rescue his people
out of respect—or out of love?
Joe Meek shackled our wrists—
but our people were saved.

When we reached Oregon City
we were all chained together, each to

each other so we could not escape
our trial, our death.

A priest came to visit us.
He baptized us all Catholic
so we at least escaped
Whitman's god.

We asked for sweet grass
and sagebrush and dry, sunny air.
We burned holy cedar.

2. *History Says*

History says only what the victor wants
remembered. No one asks the vanquished.
Why did the United States declare Oregon

a Territory eighteen months later? To get
blood vengeance on five Cayuse men
for the massacre at the Whitman Mission.

Laws were required. White men, their white
wives and white children required protection
from the red savages who lived on the land,

who *were* the land until guns and disease
and greed stole it from them.

3. I, Tomahas, Now Known as the Murderer, Will Speak No More

We were not allowed to tell our story
we were not allowed to tell why
the Doctor Marcus Whitman had to die.

No one spoke for the Cayuse way of life,
for our laws, for our customs.

We were chained and shackled.
No one brought us sunlight
or brought us dry air or sagebrush.
We shivered with the cold,
the constant damp, the wet air.
We could hardly breathe.

The white men argued
the translators talked from
English to Chinook Wawa
and back again.

We were called cowards
for defending our ways
for defending our families
for defending our children.

We five, chained and shackled,
sat and said nothing. We shivered,
but not with fear. Shackled
we stood and heard our fate.

Ten days later,
we climbed the steps
and stood where directed.
The hangman placed strong
ropes around our necks.

The priest, Father Veyret
said a prayer that meant nothing to us,
told us we'd meet again in some Heaven
the white man claims to believe in.

Marshall Joe Meek gave the order—

4. Father Veyret Remembers

The bodies were dumped in a flat bed wagon
driven out to an unmarked grave.

These five men, no longer shackled, were thrown
without respect or ceremony into an unmarked grave.

I stood at the edge, said prayers for their souls, sprinkled Holy
    Water
and threw the first dirt. I wished I could have burned sagebrush and
    sweet grass.

Why did you surrender? I asked of dead Tomahas.
His ghost whispered in my ear:

> *Does a Savior rescue his people*
> *out of respect—or out of love?*

The wind picked up as I rode away.
I smelled sweet grass and sagebrush.

I heard the thunder of ghost horses
as they raced home. Rain hid my tears.

For I, Joe Stanfield, Have Sinned

The grave is too shallow;
the wolves will come, but I
would be gone. I bathed the bodies,
I wrapped them, I stayed out
in the wind and the freezing rain.
What more could I do?

Forgive me, Father
—it's not my fault the Cayuse listened
to the lies of Joe and Nicolas. I even
married the widow Hays just to save her life.

Yes, I stole some jewelry and money
from the dead—they had no use for it.
Yes, I stole money or goods from some
of the survivors, too. After all, they owed me
for food and firewood I brought them.

And yes, when convicted, I stole
the chance when it came to escape
—leaving my wife a widow again,
though she left me first, as soon as
she was rescued.

Now, alone in the California
gold fields I will die, too.

Forgive me, Father, for I have sinned.

Alice Clarissa

On quiet nights, Narcissa
visits the little grave where
she strains to hear the voice
of her daughter crying to come home.

When Narcissa herself lies
on the cold, wet Waiilatpu ground
her life's blood draining
out of her body, the small,

cold, ghostly arms
of Alice Clarissa twine
around Narcissa's neck
as she whispers words

no one else can hear.
Many wonder if Alice Clarissa
speaks to her mother
in Cayuse or English.

Might Alice Clarissa, called
Cayuse Girl by the Indians,
have been a living bridge
between the two cultures,

if she had lived?
Might the massacre
have been avoided?

On quiet nights if you listen
with your open heart,

you may hear the winds of Waiilatpu
carry the mournful cries of

Alice Clarissa,
Cayuse Girl.

Holy Water

Grandfather Sky sends rain to baptize the earth below.
Grandmother Earth receives his blessing, covers herself in
rye grass and sagebrush. She plants fruits for all who
walk upon her, and call her home.

Nothing she sends forth is wasted, for she receives
with open hands the holy rain as it falls
without benefit of priest.

At the end of November, the rains at Waiilatpu come hard and cold,
come with a fury, soak all who dare lie down without shelter.
The winds at Waiilatpu chill the living to the depth of their bones,
churn dirt and dust to frozen mud.

Death or redemption rush down from the mountains, ride
the winds, and Grandmother Earth opens herself to receive
on her blessed ground the blood
of those who die, the bones of those now dead,
the tears of those who are left alive.

Years pass. Wild rye gives way to wheat, then grapes,
sagebrush grows only at the edges of fields in soil dry
enough that it will not drown. Wild rye, purple

in its summer bloom, still flourishes at Waiilatpu,
blessed by Grandfather's holy tears, and held
in the comfort of Grandmother's bosom.

Requiem aeternam dona eis, Domine; Et lux perpetua luceat eis.
Requiescant in pace. Amen.

(Eternal rest grant unto them, O Lord; and let perpetual light shine
    upon them.
May they rest in peace. Amen.)

BURIED IN THE GREAT GRAVE

Marcus Whitman
Narcissa Prentiss Whitman
Crockett A. Bewley
Isaac Gillen
Jacob D. Hall
Jacob Hoffman
Nathan Kimball
Walter (?) Marsh
Andrew Rogers, Jr.
Francis Sager
John Sager
Lucien Francis Saunders
Amos Sales

BURIED AT THE BASE OF THE HILL PLACE UNKNOWN

Alice Clarissa Whitman
b. Mar 14, 1837
d. June 23, 1839

Age: 2 years, 3 months, 9 days (drowned)

Notes on People and Places in Order of Appearance

Mary Ann Bridger, daughter of Jim Bridger and his Indian wife, Cora Insala.

Joe Meek, a mountain man and first U. S. marshal to the Oregon Territories.

Narcissa Prentiss Whitman, one of the first two white women (the other, Eliza Spalding) to cross the Rocky Mountains to the Oregon Country. A missionary, she was martyred on 29 November 1847.

Helen Mar Meek, daughter of Joe Meek and his Indian wife, Mountain Lamb.

Alice Clarissa Whitman, the first white baby born in the Oregon Country. She drowned at age 2 years, 3 months, 9 days. The exact site of her grave is unknown, but could be seen from the kitchen window of the Whitman home.

Joe Lewis, a man of Negro and Indian parentage, came from Canada by way of Maine. He was an angry man, who hated white people, and emigrants. The prime agitator of the massacre, he came, he caused trouble, and he disappeared.

Nicholas Finlay, a *métis* (French Canadian father, Indian mother), was one of three inciters of the massacre.

David Malin Cortez, son of a Spanish trapper and probably of a Walla Walla Indian, was another of the adopted Whitman children, and was taken, along with the Manson boys, to Fort Walla Walla at the time of the massacre.

Fort Walla Walla, located at the confluence of the Walla Walla River and the Columbia River, at the town of Wallula. The original fort and town are now under Lake Wallula, a direct result of the building of the McNary Dam.

Joe Stanfield, *métis*, was the third inciter to the massacre though he must have had second thoughts, as he stayed to help survivors and bury the dead.

Tomahas, the Cayuse who brought the mortal blow from behind to kill Marcus Whitman.

Tiloukaikt, the Cayuse who engaged Marcus in conversation to distract him from Tomahas.

John Sager, one of the adopted children, was next to Dr. Whitman during the attack. He was killed, as was his brother, Francis. The youngest Sager girl died days later from the measles. The four older girls survived. The Whitmans had adopted the seven Sager orphans, and fostered several other children. It is believed they had a total of 10 children at the time of the massacre, but it may have been 12 if the two Manson boys were included. Adoption at that time and place did not entail name changes, or legal papers. It was more closely related to what we today call foster parenting.

Father Brouillet, one of the Catholic priests trying to make inroads with the Nez Perce and Cayuse. He also baptized and helped bury the dead.

Five Crows, a young chief of the Cayuse, living near the confluence of the Umatilla and Columbia Rivers.

Lorinda Beweley, a young girl tricked by Five Crows into marriage.

Frank and **Edward (a son of Tiloukaikt)**, two Indian men who took white girls as wives.

Susan Kimball and **Mary Smith**, white girls forced into marriage with Frank and Edward.

Bishop Blanchet, Bishop of Walla Walla and to Father Brouillet.

Mrs. Hays, a young widow who thwarted Joseph Stanfield's attempt at marriage by placing her child between them in bed.

Father Veyret, the Catholic priest who not only baptized the five Cayuse Indians, but stood with them on the scaffolding as they dropped to their deaths, bringing whatever comfort he could. Thirteen men were offered to the U.S. Marshall, one for each killed, but only the five were taken.

Notes on Pronunciation

Waiilatpu – Wah-EE-lat-poo

Tomahas – Ta-MAH-hoss

Tiloukaikt – Till-OH-kaykt (like *kite* but with the extra *k* sound)

About the Author

Lenora Rain-Lee Good was born and raised in the Pacific Northwest. Her grandfather introduced her to the history of her region and her country at an early age in a manner that made it both real and alive. She hopes you find her poetry both real and alive.

Lenora now lives in Kennewick, Washington, not very far from the Whitman Mission, which she loves to visit. She shares her home with a small dog, a large cat, and a room full of quilting fabrics. She tries to divide her time between the writing of stories and the making of quilts.

Her poetry has appeared in numerous hard copy and online magazines, two of her radio dramas have been produced and aired, and she has published four Young Adult/Adult novels: *My Adventures as Brother Rat*, *Jiang Li: Warrior Woman of Yueh*, *Yadh, the Ugly*, and *Madame Dorion: Her Journey to the Oregon Country*.

www.LenoraRainLeeGood.com

For other titles available from redbat books, please visit:
www.redbatbooks.com

Also available through Ingram's, Amazon.com,
Barnesandnoble.com, Powells.com and by special order
through your local bookstore.

www.ingramcontent.com/pod-product-compliance
Lightning Source LLC
Chambersburg PA
CBHW020959090426
42736CB00010B/1389